33288076624560

D1500953

THE SPIRIT OF TEA

Introduction

Sen Sôshitsu XV

People all over the world feel strong attachments to and are proud of their cultures. In my quest to spread the way of tea throughout the world, I have come into contact with people of many countries, and from my experiences I have learned that what the people of all countries yearn for most is a spirit that embraces peace.

Recently, there have been too many heart-breaking, unspeakable events. These events have occurred not just in Japan, but elsewhere as well. It is terrible if we cannot trust even our own flesh and blood. If we go on this way, I fear, we will lose our very nature as human beings. Unless something is done, this country—indeed, this planet—may perish. Because of my strong feelings about what is happening, feelings that are like an anguished cry, I have decided to write this book.

The tea spirit is the spirit of peace, and the culture of tea is a culture of hospitality. Tea is a means for establishing and maintaining good relations among people. The tea spirit should not be confined to the tearoom. It is a spirit essential for people living together in the great world of nature with many other living beings.

"Face harmonious, words loving"—it is one of my favorite sayings. When one receives a bowl of tea from a host who has poured his feelings and spirit into the preparation of it, one cannot help but smile. I wish to spread this spirit and this wonderful culture to people throughout the world and, with a smiling face, to continue living with mutual recognition of and respect for others. Thus have I wished during these past fifty years. I will never forget the smiling face of a Russian woman as she drank a bowl of tea I had prepared for her; and I well recall the wonderful taste of tea diligently prepared for me by a Chinese youth by the sweat of his brow.

This book contains, in condensed form, things that I have been saying for years. My brother, Naya, has provided appropriate commentary. This is the first time we have produced a book together. The photographer Mr. Inoue Takao has taken splendid photographs to accompany the text.

It is my wish that the spirit of tea be transmitted, through this book, to as many people as possible throughout the world.

Table of Contents

To Receive Tea With Relish

The way of tea teaches the beauty of the finest of human relations in the offering
and acceptance of a bowl of tea.
I like to think that the mutual understanding of how to serve and receive tea
will guide people in extending the joys of today throughout their lives.
Therefore, do not refrain from partaking of tea by saying
"I don't care for any."
Instead, please accept a bowl of tea by saying
"Well, I'll give it a try."

A Bowl of Tea

These lines appear in the old text called *Sôjinboku*:

"In drinking tea, one should drink as though one were quietly taking a 'bite' at a time.

If one takes big swallows, the tea's flavor cannot be cherished.

But the last swallow should be a big one so that no dregs are left in the bowl.

Takeno Jôô said that he wanted to drink tea all day, so long as it did not get cold."

Today, we tend to drag worldly commotion into the tearoom.

We need to provide more places where we can leisurely take time to taste a bowl of tea

prepared by our host.

How wonderful it would be if we Japanese, by cherishing a bowl of tea,

could convey our spirit to the people of the various countries of the world,

perhaps to promote peace.

The Way of Drinking Tea

Sôjinboku

This is a book on the way of tea published in 1626 during the early Tokugawa period. Of unknown authorship, it is divided into three volumes. Volume one, entitled "*Gyôyô*," includes 131 rules to be followed by the host and guests at a tea gathering; volume two introduces drawings of the rooms of various tea masters; and volume three presents "instructions for the *daisu* portable stand," including styles of decorating the *daisu* in twenty-four ways (divided into three sections of eight each). The volume also contains anecdotes and the like. *Sôjinboku* is a compilation of earlier writings on tea, and is noteworthy as the first book printed on this subject. The title *Sôjinboku* is derived from the Chinese character for tea, *cha*, which comprises three components: *sô* (grass), *jin* (person), and *boku* (wood).

Ostentatious Behavior

There are many people who wonder
why such ostentatious procedures must be
employed simply to prepare a bowl of tea.
But nowhere else in the world do
we find a beverage like powdered tea (*matcha*)
that is offered by one person and received by
another in such a spirit of mutual gratitude.
Indeed, it is this handling of tea that teaches
all religious lessons to serve as guideposts
to people in their lives.
I hope that people will, in light of this,
begin to understand the purpose of
these "ostentatious" procedures in the preparation
and serving of tea.

Ways of Bowing

Bows can be divided into *zarei*, seated bows, and *ryûrei*, standing bows,
and each can be subdivided into three styles, generally recognized as: the
most respectful form of bow (*shin*), the polite bow (*gyô*), and the slight
bow (*sô*). These styles can, in turn, be identified as the bow exchanged
between guests (*tsugirei*), the received bow (*ukerei*), and the bestowed
bow (*okurirei*).

Do Foreigners Understand the Way of Tea?

I am frequently asked this question.

To me there is no difference, in the spirit of the way of tea,

between Japanese and foreigners.

Indeed, there are a great many Japanese who do not understand tea spirit;

and on the other hand, there are many foreigners who are passionate

about tea and who, in fact, pursue the way with great devotion.

With knowledge of this fact, I feel no difference between East and West,

at least so far as the way of tea is concerned.

Ikebana (flower arrangement) and other arts have already become internationalized.

Thus flowers can be found fashionably arranged and displayed in

stores and homes wherever one goes, and they have come to occupy

a place in the lives of many people. There are, of course,

some differences between the way of flowers and the way of tea.

But the idea that the way of tea is just for

Japanese and is incomprehensible to foreigners is no longer warrantable.

Foreigners and the Way of Tea

When inquiring into the introduction of the way of tea to the world outside Japan, one must cite Okakura Tenshin's *Book of Tea*, published in 1906. But the records also show that there were foreigners who began formal study of the way of tea in 1905. Three sisters—Helen, Grace, and Florence Scotfield—asked the thirteenth grand master of Urasenke, Ennôsai, to instruct them in tea and their request was granted. There remains a photograph of the sisters, dressed in formal, five-crested kimono, engaged in tea practice.

Tea was introduced to Japan from China. We can assume that it was brought by the official missions to China sometime during the Nara to early Heian periods. Lu Yü wrote the *Classic of Tea* (*Chakyô*) during this age—the age of T'ang—and the tea imported from T'ang to Japan at this time was prepared from what was called *dancha* or brick tea.

Later in China, during the Sung period, the method of preparing and drinking tea changed from the infused process using brick tea to that of dissolving powdered tea in hot water. The Zen priest Eisai (or Yôsai), who studied in Sung China and brought tea seedlings and tea methods back to Japan, wrote a text called *Kissa Yôjôki*. which explains the healthful benefits of drinking tea. After Eisai presented tea as a medicine to the shogun Minamoto Sanetomo, tea drinking speread among Zen temples. He divided the tea plants he had brought from China with his friend Priest Myôe, who planted them at Toganoo in the mountains to the west of what was then the city of Kyoto. Because the tea of Toganoo came to be regarded as the most excellent of teas, it was called *honcha* or "real tea", and the tea from other regions was known as *hicha* or "non-tea."

Heartily drunk in the beginning by Zen priests, tea gave rise to rules (*sarei*) for its usage, and tea-drinking gradually spread also among members of the warrior class. In the mid-Muromachi period Murata Shukô (or Jukô), in conjunction with the Zen priest Ikkyû of Daitokuji Temple, converted the tea rules that had until then been followed in Zen temples to the formal rules of *chanoyu*. When the shogun of that time, Ashikaga Yoshimasa, was introduced to Shukô's *chanoyu* by his attendant cultural aide (*dôbôshû*), he enthusiastically adopted it, and from then on *chanoyu*, which had only been practiced among a small group of people, spread out to the Japanese populace in general.

After Shukô, leadership in the world of tea was assumed by men from Sakai. One of these was Takeno Jôô, who further simplified Shukô's tea, promoting *wabi*-style "hut (*sôan*) tea" utilizing the small room instead of *chanoyu* in a *shoin*-style room. Sen no Rikyû inherited the spirit of Jôô's *wabicha*.

Rikyû advanced, as the way of tea, the spiritual side of *chanoyu* as it had been practiced up until his time. Moreover, in regard to the articles employed, he created the form of *chanoyu* we see today by moving beyond just the use of "Chinese pieces" (*karamono*) and employing also articles made in Japan and those from the Korean peninsula. Because Rikyû's tea was esteemed by the two leading military leaders of the time, Oda Nobunaga and Toyotomi Hideyoshi, all subsequent schools of *chanoyu* used the way of tea perfected by Rikyû as their basis and were carried on and further developed by Rikyû's descendants and disciples.

The present Sen schools of tea, representing continuity from Rikyû to his son Shôan to his grandson Sôtan, are descended from Sôtan's sons: Sôshitsu of Urasenke, Sôsa of Omotesenke, and Sôshu of Mushanokôjisenke. These Sen schools are the custodians of Rikyû's tea in a blood line from the great master himself.

Throughout the Tokugawa period the way of tea was dominated by men. But it came to be widely spread among the people in general by the idea in the early Meiji period of the eleventh Grand Master of Urasenke, Gengensai, to establish a form of *chanoyu* based on the use of chairs and tables and by the later active adoption of the way of tea in school curricula and in the work place. Further, as a result of its spread overseas, *chanoyu* has came to be recognized throughout the contemporary world as a traditional form of culture representing Japan.

History of the Way of Tea

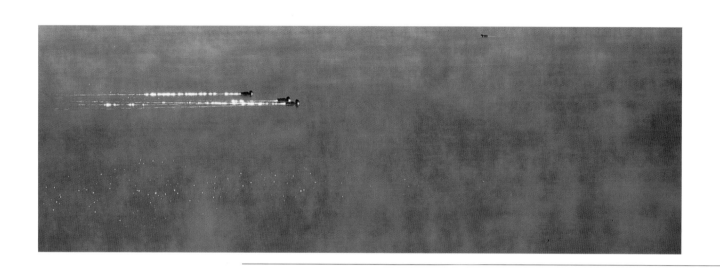

What is Tea Practice?

A Place for Making a Shameful Show of Oneself

In a certain place for practice of the way of tea,

there hangs a plaque that reads:

"A Place Making a Shameful Show of Oneself."

Once you pass through the entranceway,

you will experience no shame,

no matter how shameful a show you may make of yourself.

The practice room is where you are trained as a human,

even as you are sharply scolded

and hesitate to humiliate yourself in the process.

The principal aim of your training is to enable you,

when the time comes,

to perform tea splendidly and without shame.

This is the reason why those who pass through the entranceway

of this place are prepared to endure severe discipline.

For it is in this way that

they gradually develop fine characters as people.

They cannot achieve this simply by reading books

and listening to others.

They must experience it through their own bodies.

The way of tea, *chadô*, must be acquired by means of the movements of
your own body and through one's own experiences.
It cannot be learned by observing and listening to others and thus by imitating them.
There is no other method than this in pursuing *chadô*.
My predecessor as Grand Master impressed upon me
that the only way to learn tea was through the movements of my own body
and by accumulating experiences and storing them within my body.
Moreover, your motivation for learning tea must gush forth from within you;
it cannot be forced by others.

The Way of Tea

When you pursue the way of tea from your own solicitude, your daily practice will not end as mere practice. Rather, your practice of a certain procedure for preparing tea or the lessons you learn concerning the movements of a guest will straightaway work for you in real life. My predecessor, Mugensai (Tantansai), taught that:

"Practice and the actual preparation of tea at a gathering must be the same. It is important that you call upon yourself to do what must be done and proceed."

Be determined to walk the path step by step.

You will discover within your spirit a light that will not die.

Practice

Gengensai's Rules for Practice

The injunctions in twenty articles known as the "Rules for Practice" compiled in 1856 by the eleventh Grand Master of Urasenke, Gengensai, hang in the great preparation room (ô-mizuya) at Urasenke headquarters. Beginning with the order that "There will be strict adherence to decorum, and unnecessary talking will not be allowed," the articles include surprisingly detailed instructions, such as: "Questions are forbidden during the preparation of tea," and "There will be no talking during practice of the Seven Special Tea Exercises (shichijishiki) except for the kazucha exercise." Still another article states that "Old and young alike should undertake practice with no sense of shame." This is the teaching that esteems learning without shame.

The fourteenth Grand Master of Urasenke, Tantansai, has, in his text Mugenshû, explained the key points to be followed by people of tea under the heading "Rules of the Way of Tea."

People today, when speaking of *chanoyu*, often refer to being "dressed up" or "showy."

Whenever I hear such comments, I am saddened.

It is certainly not our wish to be judged by our outer appearances alone.

What is important is what is in us, our spirit.

However, to speak of the spirit is vague, like groping in the dark to find the doorway

out of a room. For this reason, we have forms and procedures.

Taking the tea whisk, you immediately wash and purify it.

You fold the napkin. By carrying out the procedures correctly, you approach the spirit.

I call this "putting blood into the pattern."

Blood is a person's soul, his life. Even if you are not skilled at what you are doing,

by putting your heart and soul into it

you can combine "pattern and blood" and create "form."

Pattern and Form

Concerning the Preparation of Tea

In *temae*, the preparation of tea,

you bring the utensils of tea to the mats of the tea room and place them in the correct positions.

You then prepare tea, handling the utensils according to the prescribed rules.

Great beauty is already created within the tea room by the arrangement of utensils for use.

It then becomes essential, as you move and handle the utensils in performing *temae*,

to present the most beautiful forms possible in the use of the utensils and

the preparation of tea. In the movements of *temae*, some are slow and some are fast.

Some movements are so light that they appear to be pauses

during which you seem to be holding your breath; there are also delicate movements.

This is the beauty of movement, of a sequence of beautiful forms.

However, *temae* is not simply a matter of learning such forms.

In taking the tea bowl, you must possess the spirit of taking;

in purifying the scoop, the spirit of purifying; in preparing tea, the spirit of preparing.

Only when this depth and richness of spirit is added, will it become a good *temae*.

The Beauty of Movement

Types of *Temae*

The eleventh Grand Master of Urasenke, Gengensai, in 1856
published a book entitled *Hogobusuma* that introduced to the public
to the steps for performing *temae*. The book described more than
850 kinds of *temae* and methods for handling tea utensils. It would
be difficult to measure the full extent of the influence of Gengensai's
public disquisition on *temae* in the modernization of *chanoyu*.

A person's learning of the forms may be slow and his movements may be awkward.

But when a guest observes the temae of that person who, even so, purifies the bowl with the full spirit of his heart and prepares tea with the same spirit,

he will be moved with emotion and automatically raise the tea bowl to his head in gratitude.

This is because the etiquette for the preparation of tea differs from other kinds of etiquette.

We may say that success in the preparation of tea is achieved by a combination of spirit and form.

It is not simply a matter of "appearance." Forms have been established as the bases of *temae*.

If you study and learn them correctly, there will emerge, before you know it, a tea spirit.

As the forms become part of your very being, the spirit that has just been created will be further nourished.

The etiquette of *temae* is not limited to the tea room.

It will become an integral part of your daily life.

The forms and spirit you acquire through your training will possess an appeal that will enable you to move people everywhere.

The way of tea is a powerful force in the molding of human character.

The Spirit and Form of *Temae*

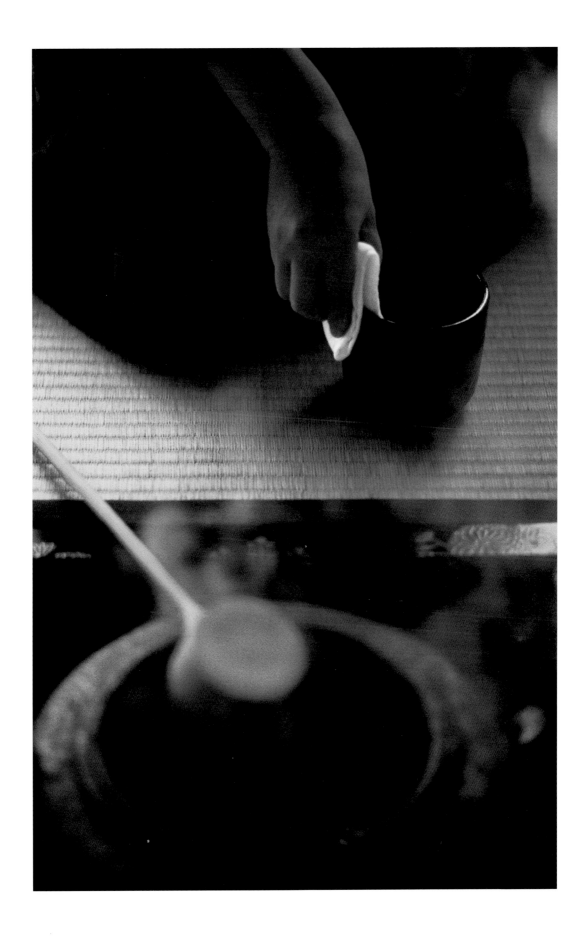

In order to prepare delicious tea,

it is extremely important to control the temperature of the hot water.

The precisely right temperature is achieved by building the fire in three stages: lighting the fire;

the first laying of charcoal (*shozumi*); and the second laying of charcoal (*gozumi*).

The laying of charcoal in the sunken hearth (*ro*) is an especially elegant procedure.

First, you purify the inside of the hearth and spread moist ash evenly in it.

You then place three sticks of ignited cylinder-shaped charcoal on the ash to start the fire.

By the time you have greeted your guests and are ready to perform the first laying of charcoal,

these three sticks of charcoal should be covered with a thin layer of ash.

Aiming for this point, you lay the charcoal.

If the starter fire is weak and the hearth is not warm,

this may be taken as a reflection of the coldness of your spirit.

The sincerity of your spirit toward your guests will be seen as inadequate.

Creating a good starter fire is more difficult than laying the charcoal.

The Condition of the Starter Fire

Types of Charcoal

The charcoal used in *chanoyu* is cut charcoal, made from a kind of oak called *kunugi*. There are differences in the charcoal for the sunken hearth and for the brazier. The best quality charcoal is produced in Ikeda City in the Ôsaka area. Charcoal is named according to its various uses: *kôgôdai*, upon which the incense container is placed; *makurazumi* and *dôzumi*, which serve as pillows for other kinds of charcoal; *gitchô*; *warigitchô*; *wadô*; *kudazumi*; *warikudazumi*; *tenzumi*; *edazumi*; and others. Charcoal used in the hearth is longer than that used in the brazier, and there are some differences in the way it is arranged. Also, *edazumi* differs from other kinds of charcoal. *Edazumi* is branch-shaped charcoal made from the burnt branches of the azalea, and is called white charcoal because it is painted with lime.

The most important features of *temae* are: the positioning of the articles,

the sequence of procedures, and the actual movements. Once the positioning is established,

there are important rules governing the sequence of procedures.

If you neglect these, you cannot properly perform *temae*.

As you make the sequence of procedures part of you, you must also concentrate on the way

you perform the movements—for example, the tempo is important.

This is called *jo, ha, kyû* (slow, medium, fast).

During *temae*, you must be spontaneously decisive in your timing.

This way you will avoid becoming disconcerted or flustered. Your *temae* will be comfortable,

and your movements will be resourceful.

Within the scope of any particular rule, you are free to use and move your body as you wish.

These are the three most important features of *temae*.

Three Important Features of *Temae*

What are *Jo, Ha, Kyû*?

This was originally a set of term expressing an ideal of art based on the terminology of ancient court music (*gagaku*). In *jo*, the tempo is relaxed and the movements simple. *Ha* brings an increase in tempo; the movements become more complex, and a dramatic highlight is achieved. In *kyû*, everything is rapid; the presentation is brought to an immediate climax and then to its finale. *Jo, ha, kyû* was incorporated into the literature and performing arts of the medieval age, and became associated with the three styles of *shin* (formal), *gyô* (semi-formal), *sô* (free). The *jo, ha, kyû* ideal has been adapted for *chanoyu* in the arrangement of the *temae* and the handling of the utensils. It is used in teaching the technique of slow and fast movements.

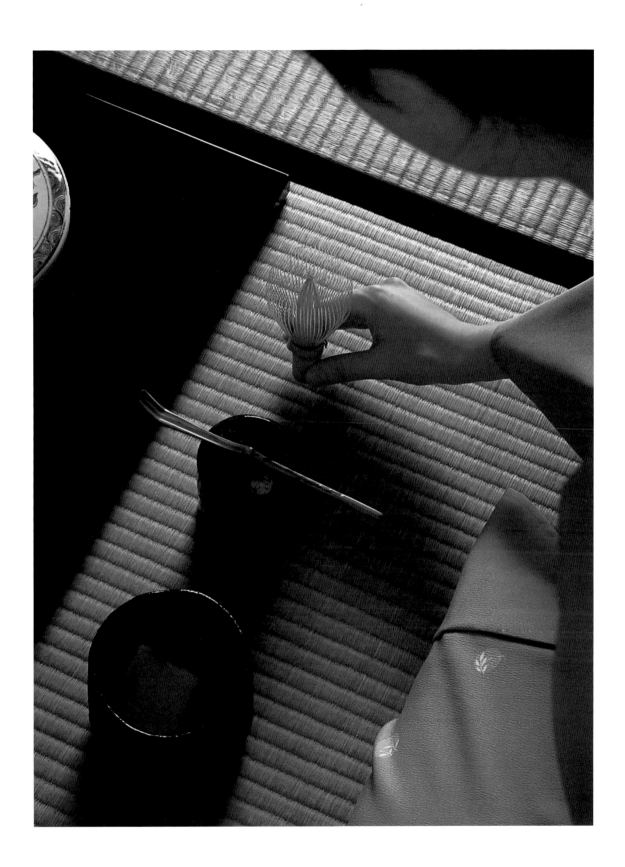

We often use the expression "One time, one meeting" (*ichigo, ichie*) in *chanoyu*.
This expression is widely used to refer to the coming together with others on a particular
occasion. But, actually, it does not imply the mere "coming together" of people and things.
The expression's real meaning lies in the extent to which
you make the most of the current moment.
A *temae* is a sequence of moments, one following the other.
Even though a certain *temae* style may always call for performance of the same set procedures,
you must train yourself to give individuality to the way you breath
and to how you handle the rhythm.

One Time, One Meeting

One Time, One Meeting

Ichigo, ichie is a phrase that expresses an ideal of the way of tea.
It first appears in *Yamanoue Sôji Ki* (*The Record of Yamanoue Sôji*), where we read: "Even though it may be an ordinary tea gathering, we must be respectful to the host—from the moment we enter the garden (*roji*) until we depart—as though it were a once-in-a-lifetime gathering." *Ichigo, ichie* later became famous because Ii Naosuke, during the last years of the Tokugawa period, repeatedly used the phrase in his *Chanoyu Ichie Shû* to explain the *chanoyu* spirit, which one must grasp.

The *temae* should never come to a standstill.

Only when you make the timing of *shu*, *ha*, *ri* (observing, breaking, abandoning) and

the knack of *jo*, *ha*, *kyû* part of yourself can you enter the realm of enlightenment

in which the *temae* and you become one.

If you dwell forever on some part of the *temae*,

you will be unable to understand either its flow or the feelings of your guests.

When you appear to be following the rules but, in fact, are not following them,

then for the first time will the profundity of your true nature as a person be revealed.

Practice the procedures of *temae* over and over, until they become yours.

You will then achieve a flow that knows no attachment to things and is boundless.

As Though Flowing

Concerning *Shu, Ha, Ri*

This was originally a set of military terms that was adopted into *chanoyu* to express the series of stages in practicing tea. In the first stage, *shu*, one carefully observes the rules of *chanoyu* and absorbs them. In the second stage, *ha*, one breaks away from the rules; and finally, one reaches the stage (*ri*) of releasing the rules altogether to enter a realm of free expression. There is a teaching poem (*dôka*) that says, in regard to the rules and methods of chanoyu, that once you have observed them thoroughly, you should not forget their essences, even though you break away and release them.

The terms *shu*, *ha*, *ri* have also been used to interpret the degree of skill attained in tea practice: *shu* represents the stage of the unskilled, *ha* that of the skilled, and *ri* is the stage of the master (*meijin*).

We are told that the ladle was first made by a bowyer, and the handling of the ladle appears to have been adapted from the way of the bow and arrow.

Thus, you perform the *okibishaku* method of placing the ladle down with the same feeling as nocking an arrow to a bowstring.

The *hikibishaku* method is done with the sense that you are drawing the bow into the shape of a full moon. And in the *kiribishaku* method, you must express the feeling one has when suddenly releasing an arrow into flight. A weak hand will spoil the movement of the ladle.

The key points in handling the ladle are that you must have strength in the abdomen and be completely relaxed, using a lightness of touch. If one's fingers are stiff, it is difficult for the hand to move freely and one's movements will appear awkward.

The Ladle and the Bow and Arrow

The Ladle (*Hishaku*)

Made of bamboo, the ladle is a utensil used for scooping both hot and cold water. It consists of two parts: the cup and the handle. If the handle extends into the cup, the ladle is called a *sashitôshi*. Such a ladle is used without distinction with both the sunken hearth and the portable brazier. Another type of ladle is the *kiridome*, whose handle is cut diagonally at the tip. If the fleshy side of the bamboo is cut this way, the ladle is for use with the brazier. If the side with the skin is cut, the ladle is for use with the sunken hearth.

Concerning Host and Guest

If it were simply a matter of *temae* and preparing tea, anyone could do that.

After the guests have partaken of their sweets and you judge the time to be just right,

you serve tea and your guests receive it from you.

To refer to the time as "just right" is, of course, to speak of timing.

You may make mistakes in the *temae* and your utensils may not be of the highest quality;

but if you prepare the tea whole-heartedly and offer it to your guests with sincerity of spirit,

the bowls will truly be bowls of noble tea.

And, thus, the guests can receive and drink the tea in the sincerity of their own spirits.

Noble Tea

Sottaku Dôji (the Coordination of Crying and Pecking)

Sotsu is the cry of the baby chick within its shell trying to get out, and *taku* is the pecking on the outside of the shell by the parent bird because it has heard the chick's cry. We are told in an old story that when the crying and pecking occur at the same time, the chick will be born. This is exactly how it is with the timing between host and guests and between guests.

Preparing Tea Just Right

In *chanoyu*, the host invites his guests into the tea room and,
by employing the rather complicated procedures of *temae*,
expresses his feelings of sincerity toward them.
If you should feel, in observing just the *temae* procedures,
that they are formal and far-fetched,
you will not be able to demonstrate the true way of tea.
Rikyû once casually enjoined us to "Prepare tea just right."
Unless everything is done correctry
—the utensils harmoniously matched,
the temperature of the hot water adjusted,
the proper amount of tea measured,
the tea whisk handled correctly, and so forth—
your preparation of tea will not be "just right."

Seven Rules

Seven rules passed down to us by Rikyû are:
1. Arrange flowers as they are in the fields.
2. Lay charcoal so the water boils.
3. Keep cool in the summer.
4. Stay warm in the winter.
5. Be early.
6. Be prepared for rain even if it is not raining.
7. Be mindful of the guests.

So long as the house does not leak and the food is sufficient to stave off hunger—

these are the teachings of the Buddha and the true purpose of *chanoyu*.

You fetch water, gather firewood, heat the water, and prepare tea.

You offer some tea to the Buddha, serve your guests, and drink of the tea yourself.

Arranging flowers, burning incense—

all are part of learning the way of the Buddha as it has come down to us (*Nanpôroku*).

In teaching about such things, Rikyû seems to have had as his true purpose a return to nature.

Of course, nature in this sense does not mean just the natural elements,

such as the rain, wind, and clouds. It includes also people

who have discovered their true selves, who have returned to their true natures—

in short, it is nature conceived as all of creation.

When, through daily practice and accumulated learning, you finally come to understand,

there will be revealed to you the most human of forms.

It will be the form of the true person of tea.

Herein lies the ideal of the way of tea.

Returning to Nature

Nanpôroku

Nanpôroku is one of the most important of the secret texts we have for understanding Rikyû's tea. It comprises seven sections: *Oboegaki* (memoranda), *Kai* (gatherings), *Tana* (shelves), *Shoin* (a style of room), *Daisu* (lacquered stands), *Sumibiki* (ink trailings), and *Metsugo* (after death). Some would add *Hiden* (secrets) and *Tsuika* (addenda) to bring the total of sections to nine. Research has yet to provide solid conclusions about the writing and textual history of *Nanpôroku*. But from the Tokugawa period this work has made a great contribution to the advancement of the way of tea, and has unquestionably become a conceptual basis for it. *Nanpôroku* informs us about how to set the utensils out harmoniously (*kanewari*) and the ideal of *wabicha* (tea based on the *wabi* aesthetic) and is rich in anecdotes about Rikyû.

If tea, like the moon at its clearest,

could promote a beautiful state of mind in people throughout the world,

it would surely make a great contribution to world peace.

After the war, a reporter of United Press International visited our tea house.

I invited him into the tea house and immediately served him tea.

After a tranquil period of time together, I asked what he thought of the tea.

He replied that,

although he was still far from understanding the spirit of tea,

he wondered if it might not be likened to

the soundless sound of the moon rising in the sky.

The Spirit of
the Moon

People of old taught us that "To be fulfilled is good; to wish to be fulfilled is bad."

The trouble is that, in today's world of tea, all too many tea gatherings and events are conducted superficially with host and guests seeking to be "fulfilled."

The spirit of fulfillment will arise naturally.

It is unnecessary to think "I'll do that for them. That's what I'm going to do!"

If your utensils are insufficient, then they are insufficient.

But if you arrange them properly and in a skillful way and are sensitive in dealing sincerely with your guests, a spirit of fulfillment will arise.

Moreover your guests, disregarding the special feeling

they may have at being invited or called upon to be your guests,

will also surely experience a spirit of fulfillment upon becoming aware that

they have been drawn into their host's realm of sincerity.

The Spirit of Fulfillment

Why Does One Turn the Tea Bowl?

In Urasenke *chanoyu*, one turns the tea bowl twice clockwise before drinking, although it does not really matter which direction you turn the bowl or even how many times you turn it. The host presents the bowl with its most beautiful side to the front. By arranging to have this side face the guest, the host extends his courtesy to him. The guest, with a sense of humility, deliberately turns the bowl in order to avoid drinking from the front and thus to show his sincerity and respect in response to the host's consideration.

Society is an extension of personal relations, and we respect good sense as a means
for lubricating such relations.

There is no need to be a splendid person or an eminent person.

If you have a gentle spirit and are not lacking in good sense, no further display is necessary.

For those of us who devote ourselves to tea, it is the inner being,
not the outer appearance, that is most important.

Behind the procedures of *temae* lies the already mature spirit of tea.

When you are strict in your thinking, you will possess a means for reflection,
and there will emerge in the pressed earth the sprout of a harmonious heart.

It is my wish that each and every person who studies the way of tea will have hung, within himself, a scroll reading "harmonious spirit."

I hope that, before you speak, exercise your intellect, or voice your emotions, you will silently unroll that scroll for yourself.

The Harmonious Spirit

What are *Wa, Kei, Sei, Jaku* (Harmony, Respect, Purity, Tranquility)?

Rikyû summarized the four principles of the essence of the way of tea in four words: *wa* (harmony), *kei* (respect), *sei* (purity), and *jaku* (tranquility). *Wa* is the basis for the commonality of all people. Through it, people acknowledge each other, yield to one another, and bring each other together in groups. *Kei* is the recognition by both host and guests of their mutual worthiness of respect as individuals; reverence toward other people. *Sei* means not only physical cleanliness, but also purification of the spirit and acting freely in accordance with that spirit. *Jaku* refers to the serene and steadfast state of mind whose spirit is not shaken by change. Nirvana (*nehan*), the world of ultimate peace and harmony.

The host must be a producer.

At the same time, he must enter the spirit of the guests

who come to receive tea from him and reflect therein upon his deportment.

Taking care to avoid anything indiscrete, he arranges everything, starting with the tea utensils,

in accordance with his experience and within his means.

As for the rest of the production, the host induces the guests to join him in piecing it out.

This is the key to the host's role.

Only when the guests understand this fact and come privately to appreciate the host's spirit

will a true appreciation of their human relationship—deep human relations—arise.

The Deportment of the Host

Observing

By observing everything that makes up a tea event or gathering, the guest comes to understand the host's consideration for him. This refers not to just the utensils, but also to the arrangement of the tea room, the maintenance of the garden, and the atmosphere of the gathering—in short, to everything. The guest views these things in sequence during the flow of the gathering. It is no exaggeration to say that the true flavor of *chanoyu* is the combination of, on the one hand, the capacity of the guests to discern the host's spirit and, on the other hand, of the host's concern for his guests and his ability to express himself in entertaining them.

Rikyû has taught us: "When entertaining a guest, treat him as you would a nobleman."

Take no notice of his status or position.

Show him a spirit of respect without any sense of discrimination,

as though both you and he were naked.

Isn't respect for people something to be welcomed? I believe its basis lies in courtesy.

As people are of service to one another, there arises a mutual happiness.

The characters used to write *tsukaeau*,

"to be of service to one another," can also be read as *shiawase* or "happiness."

Thoughtfulness is a means for showing your spirit.

However, if you are too obviously thoughtful, too pushy, or too forceful,

your guest will beat a hasty retreat.

It is important that your thoughtfulness be unobtrusive.

Respecting People

The Procedure for Serving Noblemen (*Kinindate*)

Among Urasenke's "Sixteen Things to Learn" is *kinindate* or "Tea Procedure for Serving Noblemen." This is performed when you invite your teacher or someone you highly respect to tea. Whether it is thick tea or thin tea, you serve one bowl per guest. You also serve sweets on pedestaled lacquer dishes (*takatsuki*), one per guest. The purpose of *kinindate* is to learn how to perform *temae* for respected guests with the proper attitude and technique.

Concerning the Tea Gathering

You must have noticed that, although it is only the bowl of tea that you have daily and that

you prepare using the same kind of tea and boiling water in the same way,

it never tastes the same. Try preparing tea once when you are angry.

When you scoop the tea into the bowl with the tea scoop

and then tap the scoop against the rim of the bowl, the bowl might break.

Or the scoop might break.

If you prepare tea when your spirit is agitated, your movements will be crude.

Yet, oddly, even at such a time, as you whip the tea smoothly with the whisk,

you will become composed. Your state of mind is readily revealed in the tea you prepare.

At the same time, you can calm your feelings as you handle the whisk. . . .

The act of preparing tea is effective in enabling you to control and reflect upon yourself.

Preparing Tea Effectively

The Quantity of Powdered Tea (*Matcha*)

The suitable amount of *matcha* to use for thin tea is one-and-a-half scoops, or about 1.9 grams, per bowl. For thick tea, use three heaping scoops, or 3.75 grams, per person. A caddy called *natsume*, containing a plentiful amount of *matcha*, is used for thin tea. Scoop out enough for one bowl. In the case of thick tea, a caddy called *chaire* is used, and the exact amount of tea for the number of guests to be served has been measured out and placed in it. You revolve the caddy and empty the contents into a bowl. The amount of water for both thin and thick tea is the same: enough for about three-and-a-half swallows per person. Because thick tea is drunk by passing the bowl among several guests, it the water naturally be measured for the right number.

The temperature of the water for thick tea should be between 75 and 85 degrees Celsius. Thin tea tastes best if the temperature is slightly lower. But since there are differences in the kinds of kettles used, the weather on particular days, the humidity, and the condition of the water, the host's expert judgment is necessary.

An Act of
This Very Moment

Tea is centered on its association with nature.

When Rikyû was summoned by his teacher Jôô to visit

Jôô's mountain village hut, it was during July at its hottest.

As Rikyû arrived at the hut with sweat pouring off him,

he was greeted by a refreshing mountain breeze.

How delighted I am to have come, Rikyû thought.

Passing through the garden (*roji*),

he noticed that a fresh green leaf had fallen onto the water

basin (*tsukubai*) at the side of the garden's path.

The leaf, he saw, was covered with dew.

At that instant Rikyû realized that tea is an act of this very moment.

It is not an act of "now," but "of this very moment"—

a moment of surprise.

Jôô placed the leaf in the water basin because, owing to the heat of summer,

the valley water in the basin would soon become lukewarm.

The lesson from this is that Jôô hoped, by floating the leaf,

to preserve an atmosphere of coolness,

and thus to transmit his feelings to Rikyû.

Here was an act "of this very moment."

If you are going to do something "resourceful" and use glassware and cut glass,

utensils that are not specifically created for the way of tea,

it may be proper to speak of what you do as "resourceful."

But if you go far beyond the rules of *chanoyu*, which evolved deep within Japanese tradition,

and employ mischievous ideas in disregard of the true intent of tea,

then your actions can never be considered "resourceful."

Moreover, such actions tend toward preoccupation with exterior forms, and by trying them

you cannot be said to have absorbed within yourself the true meaning of the way of tea.

Even in the course of your life, resourcefulness holds deep meaning and is very important.

In order to perform even a single thing,

you must be able to thoroughly understand and interpret it, and then to handle it skillfully.

Only in this way can you be resourceful.

Selecting

Selected Utensils

Articles made for other purposes that are used as utensils in *chanoyu* are called selected utensils. *Chanoyu* originally used utensils called *karamono* (Chinese articles) that were made in China. But with the rise of Rikyû, utensils made in Japan called *wamono* (Japanese articles) were selected and came to be actively used. Kôrai bowls, which are miscellaneous everyday articles from Korea that were taken into *chanoyu* for use as tea bowls, are typical examples of selected utensils.

The *kimono* is not mandatory in *chanoyu*; you may also wear Western-style clothing.

It is not the *kimono* that performs *chanoyu*, but people.

In practicing *temae*, it is permissible to wear Western clothing while you learn,

because what you are studying is the spirit of tea.

However, the formal tea gathering is a different matter. The tea room is a Japanese room,

which requires sitting on *tatami* and moving and bearing yourself in a particular manner.

With the tea room as a stage, you create something beautiful,

arranging and placing the utensils and even including your guests

among the elements of beauty.

The *kimono* must be incorporated into this setting.

The way of tea is a traditional art of Japan,

and nothing, in my opinion,

compares with the *kimono* for use in the practice of it.

The *Kimono*

The *Kimono*

Kimono for both men and women are made from the same quantity of cloth. The bolt of cloth for making one *kimono* is called *tanmono*. It is 36 to 38 centimeters in width. The length varies according to the type of kimono. For a standard *kimono*, the *tanmono* is about 12 to 12.5 meters long, although those for the summer *kimono* (*yukata*) and for *kimono* made of pongee (*tsumugi*) range from 11.5 to 12 meters. As a standard of measure for the *kimono*, the Japanese have traditionally used a ruler called *kujirajaku* with one *shaku* equaling 38 centimeters. The formal *kimono* is distinguished by a family crest (*mon*). *Kimono* are further categorized as full-dress (*yômon*) and semi-dress (*nuimon*). These are worn according to the kind of tea event and your role in it. In Japan today, the world of tea offers the greatest number of opportunities to wear *kimono*. Hence we wish to preserve the rules governing *kimono*.

Shaza kissa is an expression that means: "Well, sit down and have some tea."

People always need peace of mind.

When things happen and they get flustered and upset, many mistakes are made.

You must be prepared to deal in an ordinary way with any situation you may face.

It is for this reason that your initial preparation and final cleaning up are so important.

No matter how splendid your utensils may be, they will be useless if you are not prepared.

And if you do not clean up properly, the utensils cannot be used in the next gathering.

If you work hard and sincerely on preparing and cleaning up,

Preparing and Cleaning Up

Ennôsai's Rules for the Preparation Room (*Mizuya*)

In the great preparation room of the Totsutotsusai tea room at Urasenke in Kyoto there hangs a plaque in the hand of the thirteenth Grand Master of Urasenke, Ennôsai, listing rules for the room. In addition to a chart showing the storage places for the utensils, there is written: "This is a training ground for the tea room. Recently it has not been kept in order and has become quite unsightly. I have drawn a chart; henceforth, people who finish practicing must place all utensils back where they found them." Precisely because the preparation room is not seen by guests, it must be kept cleaner than the tea room itself.

you will naturally feel at ease and be able to devote your attention to what you are doing.
Herein lies the meaning of Rikyû's rule: "Be prepared for rain even if it is not raining."
If you are sufficiently at ease to say "Well, sit down and have a bowl of tea,"
then you will be able at any time to look inside yourself and deal with things, won't you?

Tea does not have to be prepared only in the tea room.

You can go outdoors and hold a tea gathering amid nature. This is called *nodate*.

The largest *nodate* ever held was probably Toyotomi Hideyoshi's Great Tea Gathering

at the Kitano Shrine in Kyoto. Hideyoshi had sign boards erected at street corners inviting

everyone to the Gathering, without distinction; and it is pleasant to note that

he specified they could bring whatever kettles they wished.

During cherry blossom season, one often sees tea gatherings at which large umbrellas

have been set up to protect against the sun, stands have been put in place,

and a curtain has been arranged to enclose the area.

And it seems that tea gatherings are also held under the shade of trees in the summer and on snow-covered fields in the winter. It is truly elegant to place a bright red camellia out for decoration and prepare and drink green-colored tea in the snow.

Since *nodate* is an adaptation of *chanoyu*, there are no strict rules.

It is quite free. Boxed tea utensil sets may be used, and various kinds of shelves, but *nodate* is limited to thin tea.

Preparing Tea Outdoors
Nodate

Concerning *Nodate*

Nodate refers to setting up an area for tea and performing *chanoyu* outdoors. In the old days it was called *fusube* (sooty) tea. The term *fusube* tea comes from a story of how Rikyû, visiting Hakozaki in Kyûshû, dug a hole in the ground to serve as a sunken hearth, hung a kettle from the branch of a pine tree, and, burning pine needles, prepared tea. It is also called *nogake* tea. Today, *nodate* gatherings are held using a set of portable tea utensils contained in a traveling chest (*tabi-dansu*) and a tea box (*chabako*) or a tea basket (*chakago*). Stands designed for *ryûrei chanoyu*, or tea utilizing seating furniture, are also often used in *nodate*.

Chanoyu using tables and seats is unique to Urasenke.

In addition to a table called *tenchaban*, which serves as the place where the host sets the utensils,

another table called *kikka* and round chairs (*en'i*) are provided.

This form of *chanoyu* was developed by the eleventh Grand Master of Urasenke, Gengensai,

in the early Meiji period in response to the trend of the times.

Since then, *ryûrei chanoyu*—performed

not only in Japanese rooms but also in Western-style rooms and,

at times, utilized for the sake of convenience—has been highly treasured in many quarters.

Tea Using Seating Furniture
Ryûrei

Ryûrei Stands

The *ryûrei* stand was conceived so that the host and guests could prepare and drink tea seated in chairs. The table (*tenchaban*) developed by Gengensai in 1871 is the only *ryûrei* stand that can be used for formal tea events (chaji), in which case it is assembled and used on *tatami*. Other stands are the Misonodana developed by Tantansai in 1952, the Chisindana by Hôunsai in 1968, the Shunjûdana by Hôunsai in 1971, and the *Seiwadana* of 1997.

It does not take note of the seasons, and the portable brazier is always used.
Generally speaking, it is probably correct to say that
this form of *chanoyu* is suitable to the summer. Since seats are used,
both host and guests should be careful not to slouch and to keep their legs together.

Concerning Tea Utensils

There are many tea utensils; but if you have just a bowl and whisk, you can prepare tea.

Take the can of powdered tea you bought and,

using a spoon instead of a scoop to measure tea from it into the bowl,

simply pour in hot water from your pot. By whipping the mixture with a whisk,

You will certainly have prepared tea. But there will be no beauty in it.

If, on the other hand, you should have a *natsume* tea caddy and a tea scoop,

how greatly would your spirit be enriched.

The utensils of tea are objects that gratify your spirit.

Keep them near you and you can learn much from them. Even if you do not know *chanoyu*,

you can establish a relationship with tea from just a *natsume* caddy and a tea bowl.

Utensils

The Tea Whisk (*Chasen*)

The whisk is a utensil, made of bamboo, that is used to blend and whip tea. Whisks are made from three types of bamboo: white bamboo (*shirodake*), smoked bamboo (*susudake*), and green bamboo (*aodake*). There are many varieties of whisks, depending on the number of tines and the shapes.
Whisks appear from ancient times in literary and documentary writings and in narrative picture scrolls (*emakimono*), but the style of whisk used today was first made at the request of Murata Shukô by Takayama Sôsetsu of Takayama in Yamato Province. Even today these whisks are being produced in great number in Takayama Village, Ikoma District, Nara Prefecture.

The tea scoop, which is a bamboo spatula, and the tea whisk convey
the simple beauty of folk craft. Foreigners often ask if they can buy them from us.
Scoops, along with incense containers and tea caddies,
are the utensils that guests as a rule ask to examine.
The scoop plays an important role in conveying creativity to the person of tea inasmuch as
the character, personality, refinement, and style of its maker are reflected in it.

The Tea Scoop
Chashaku

The Tea Scoop

The *chashaku* is a utensil used to scoop powdered tea. Originally, scoops were made
of ivory, tortoise shell, plain wood, and lacquered wood. But the material for scoops
changed when Murata Shukô had Shutoku make them out of bamboo. Scoops can
vary in size, but Rikyû established the scoop of about eighteen centimeters in length
as the standard. The location of the joint on a tea scoop is a matter of personal
preference. Shukô preferred a scoop without a joint; Jôô liked the joint at the
handle end; and Rikyû liked it in the middle. In the time of Sen Sôtan and Kobori
Enshû, a literary flavoring was given to scoops with the bestowal of poetic names on
them. Two and three boxes, one fitting into the other, were also made for them.
Among all the utensils of tea, the standards of quality of the scoop are the highest.
Special experience is required to judge them.

If the scoop was made by someone in ancient times,
it presents an opportunity to be touched by that person's tea virtue.
And if the scoop has a name (*mei*) given to it, the guests can appreciate
the consideration of their host as reflected in that name
and understand his intentions.

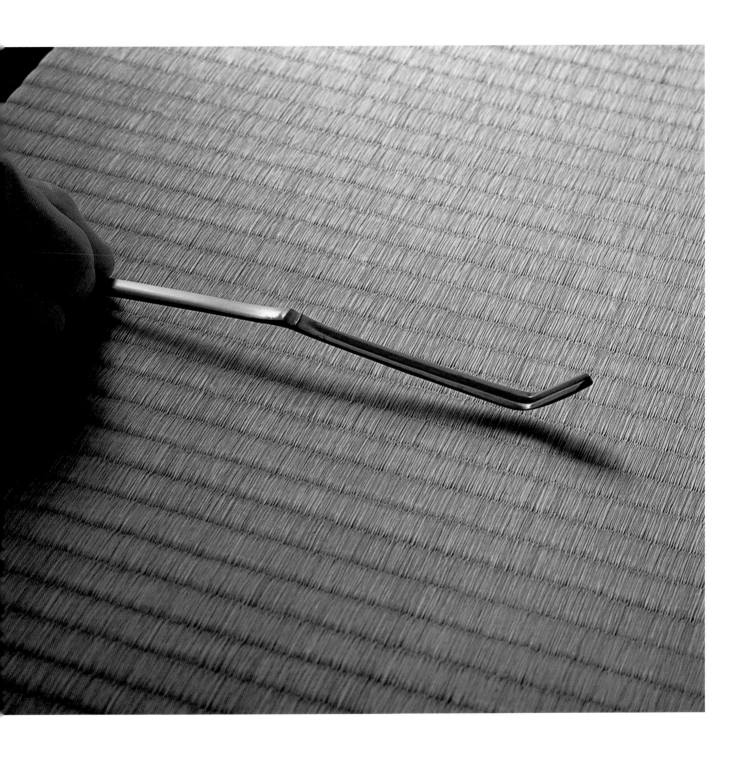

A teaching poem instructs us that your attitude in handling tea utensils should be:

"When releasing one utensil to pick up another,

think as you would if you were parting from a loved one."

No matter what utensil it may be, when in the course of your handling you change to another,

you must handle the first utensil—releasing it reluctantly—

as though you were parting from someone you loved.

I often see those who, going through the steps of *chanoyu*,

handle the utensils nonchalantly as they move easily from one to another.

Such movements are tasteless and brusque.

However, to handle the utensils with too much affection is oppressive.

It is important to acquire the knack of doing it just right.

Handling

Rikyû's Teaching Poems (*Dôka*)

The teachings of *chanoyu* and knowledge of the handling of tea utensils are presented in easily understandable form through the medium of the teaching poem. What is known as *Rikyû Koji Hyakushu* (*Master Rikyû's One Hundred Poems*) is given as *Jôô Hyakushu* (*Jôô's One Hundred Poems*) in the collection *Gunsho Ruijû*. But, in fact, neither Rikyû nor Jôô compiled these poems. They were compiled by someone in a later age, and were introduced by the eleventh Grand Master of Urasenke, Gengensai, as *Chadô Kyôyu Hyakushu Ei* (*One Hundred Poems of the Teacher of the Way of Tea*) in his *Hogobusuma*.

Hang a scroll that you like in the alcove, arrange some seasonal flowers,

and sit before the alcove and admire them.

What do you feel in the moment when you quietly gaze upon scroll and flowers?

Don't you have a sense of composure? I would like you,

even in this busy age and even though your house may be small,

to set aside a space (although it may seem a wasteful use of space) to serve as a place

where you can reflect upon yourself. An alcove is a space between people;

it is also an important space for living that brings enrichment.

When it is time to retire at night, roll up the scroll, just as you would change into

your nightclothes, and place it within the alcove, toward the side.

When you rise in the morning, you can hang the scroll again with refreshed feeling.

Although it is the same scroll,

this will bring out its freshness and the significance of hanging it in the alcove.

The Alcove
Tokonoma

The Alcove and Hanging Scrolls

I do not hesitate to say that the alcove, its historical development aside, is the most important space in the tea room; and it is of first significance for the arranging of tea utensils. The host, at the very outset, considers which scroll to hang in the alcove. With the scroll as his centerpiece, he then decides upon the other articles to be used in a tea gathering. We find confirmation of this procedure in the fact that scrolls are mentioned first in the records of tea gatherings (*kaiki*). Thus the scroll hung in the alcove plays the principal role among the articles of a tea gathering. Rikyû even went so far as to reduce the size of an alcove in order to accommodate the length of a scroll.

There is a line in a poem that reads: "Blue mountains, green waters—they are my home."

This may appear to be just another line of poetry, but it enables one to understand

the splendor of nature and how humans can merge to become one with it.

How I wish to be like the poet, so that when I am asked where I live,

I can casually answer: "The blue mountains and green waters—they are my home."

Yet, until I attain sufficient enlightenment, I cannot reply in that way.

The best I can do now is to recite the line of poetry over and over.

I close my eyes and try to conjure up blue mountains and green waters in my mind,

and I find a bowl of tea resting in my hands.

When I open my eyes and look, the bowl is full of green tea.

Within a small bowl is a great expanse of nature.

As I drink the tea quietly, the blue mountains and green waters become my home.

The Tea Bowl
Chawan

The Tea Bowl

The tea bowl is an article from which to drink tea. Because it is the only article in a tea gathering to come into contact with a guest's mouth, it is of particular importance. It is usually made of ceramic ware or porcelain, and can be roughly divided into *karamono* (produced in China), *kôraimono* (Korea), *wamono* (Japan), and *shimamono* (Southeast Asia). From olden times bowls have been esteemed by tea people. There are a great number of varieties, and many have been made by tea people themselves. These are called *tezukune* (hand molded) and *tebineri* (hand wrought), and they are greatly treasured.

Ash is a most important thing for the tea person,

and is indispensable for both the sunken hearth and the portable brazier.

Especially when using the brazier, making ash is essential training.

Always working quickly, you must create living ash.

Soon after you make a bed of ash, you must present it to your guests to view.

Always remember that "Ash is one part of tea."

When you actually make ash, you will come to understand

how difficult it is to shape so that it has a sense of life.

Learning how to shape a bed of ash is

one of the most important accomplishments of the tea person.

Living Ash

Ash and Ash Forms

Ash is one of the most important things for the person of tea. There are various kinds of ash: moist ash (*shimeshibai*) for the sunken hearth, and raw ash (*kibai*) and accompanying ash (*tomobai*) for the brazier. For the pipe lighter for the smoking set, there is caltrop ash (*hishibai*). In addition, for sprinkled ash (*makibai*), there are a great variety of types, including wisteria ash (*fujibai*) and stick-incense ash (*senkôbai*). None of these types of ash can be produced overnight. It is said that the cultivation of good ash requires at least thirty years. There are a considerable variety of ash forms used in the brazier. Of all the techniques in *chanoyu*, mastering these requires the most training. The scene that you create with ash is for the pleasure of your guests.

Concerning Tea Flowers

You cut the cleanness of the green bamboo, pour the clearness of the water, purify your spirit, and arrange the pure forms of the flowers. This is called the four purities of flowers.

Unless you appreciate the nobility of nature, the world will be totally dreary.

Within the shadow of scientific advancement and development,

you must have a self that exists vis-a-vis the natural forms of flowers. No matter who you are, you will find in this a place where you can take a deep breath and relax.

If you fiddle this way and that with the flowers and consequently they wither,

that will be of no benefit. It is the same with a person's life.

The Four Purities of Flowers

Bamboo Flower Vases

It is said that the bamboo flower vase was first used by Rikyû. Three vases purportedly made by Rikyû himself have come down to us: *Shakuhachi*, a vase simply sliced away at the top to form the mouth for the flower; the single-tiered Onjôji; and the two-tiered *Yonaga*. These are called the "three famous tubes." Of the three, *Shakuhachi* is regarded as the ultimate masterpiece among bamboo flower vases.

In one of seven rules he left, Rikyû instructs us:

"Flowers should be arranged as they are in the fields."

People cannot artificially recreate the beauty of tea flowers. They are things of life,

and have life when they reflect their forms exactly as they blossom in the fields.

This does not mean, however, that the scene of flowers

blooming in profusion in the fields should be literally replicated.

Even if it is just a single flower,

there is true significance if you arrange it in a spirit full of the flower's life.

Flowers as They are in the Fields

The *Shin, Gyô, Sô* of Flower Vases

Flower vases have various ranks, and must be handled as prescribed. The highest ranked vase is the *shin* or formal vase. Vases at this rank include Chinese and other imported bronze and celadon porcelain vases of refined shape. The lacquered board called *yahazuita* is used for *shin* vases. Among the *gyô* or semi-formal flower vases are glazed Japanese vases, including those of Seto and Tanba. For these, when placed on tatami, the lacquered *hamaguriba* board is used. Last are the unglazed flower vases, categorized as *sô* or free vases. These include: unglazed Shigaraki and Bizen vases; hand-made *Raku* ware; and bamboo vases. Unlacquered cedar and burnt-cedar boards are used for *sô* vases.

The flowers of *chanoyu* come from nature.

No matter how expensive and splendid the utensils are that you place in the tea room,

they are, after all, still-life objects.

Only the "wind blowing through the pines" sound of the kettle suggests activity.

The "movement in stillness" within the tea room, then, refers to the flowers,

which possess the fresh force of life.

Without flowers, the tea room becomes truly a place of "stillness in stillness,"

and this is an important reason why flowers are a must in the tea room.

Movement in Stillness

Prohibited Flowers

There are a number of flowers that have traditionally been regarded as unsuitable for the tea room. Among those recited as not to be placed in flower vases are: *chinchyôge*, *miyamashikimi*, *keitô*, *ominaeshi*, *zakuro*, *kôhone*, *kinsenka*, and *senreika*. Some of these flowers are, in fact, used as tea flowers today. In general, however, flowers that have unpleasant-sounding names or convey an image of inauspiciousness are considered inappropriate as tea flowers.

When arranging flowers, it is, first of all,

essential that you pour your honest spirit into the handling of them.

You must not damage their natural forms. You do not need a special technique

that requires that the flowers be arranged skillfully or that they be made to appear beautiful.

What matters is that you arrange them according to their natural features

and that they convey a sense of lingering feelings.

Don't add here and change there because the flowers somehow look solitary or lacking.

If you say absolutely everything you have to say about something,

then obviously there is nothing more to say.

What you leave unsaid—that is the charm of *chanoyu*.

Lingering Feelings

Flowers By Request

Flowers for the tea room are one of the pleasures of the host. But when the host has a treasured vase or has received flowers that were difficult to acquire or are particularly unusual, he does not arrange them himself but requests the guests to arrange them. This is what is called flowers by request, and it is in accordance with sixteen rules that serve as a guide for *temae*. When the gathering is finished and it is time to go home, it is customary for the guests to take the flowers that they arranged, wrap their stems in paper (*kaishi*), and place them in a corner of the alcove. Of course, this is all done as the occasion requires.

The Tea Room and Garden *Roji*

It is most important in our culture to harmonize with nature.

I think of the naturally twisted tree branch installed, without change,

as a post in the Japanese tea room. This is the spirit of harmonizing with nature.

It is said that, from ancient times,

the Japanese have keenly sharpened their sensibility toward nature.

This is only to be expected from a people who created the way of tea.

Let's look at Japanese architecture.

A building opens on to a garden, and the garden opens on to nature.

The Tea Room

The Composition of the Tea Room

The tea room is a structure for the practice of *chanoyu*. It is built either as an independent structure or as a unit connected to a main building. The basic compositional feature of the tea room is its layout. Its interior is divided into the host's seat (*temaeza*) and the guests' seats (*kyakuza*), which are linked by the sunken hearth. Positioned around this layout are the entrance and exit, the alcove, windows, ceiling, and the preparation room. Three remaining tea rooms that are designated national treasures are Taian, Joan, and Mittan. In addition, there are many tea rooms that are designated important cultural properties. The great majority of these are concentrated in Kyoto.

When Rikyû constructed a hut-sized (sôan) tea room, he built into it a small entranceway.

It would have been fine to have a wide opening for both entering and leaving.

Then why did he build a small entranceway?

Rikyû could not abide the troublesome rules of the feudal age

in which he lived that distinguished the statuses of those high and low

and specified that guests be allowed in according to status.

If social distinctions were always brought into the tea room,

they would completely destroy the harmonious atmosphere of tea gatherings.

So Rikyû built the small *nijiriguchi* to teach people how to set aside their statuses temporarily and behave toward one another like true human beings.

You must thus crouch down as though looking at your feet,

and in that position open the door to enter.

Rikyû taught that, in the same way that all people are born from the wombs of their mothers,

the moment you enter through the *nijiriguchi*

you will feel as though you have returned to your original state as a new-born baby.

The Crawling-In Entrance
Nijiriguchi

Concerning the *Nijiriguchi*

The *nijiriguchi* is an opening in the wall of a tea house for the entrance and exit of guests. Its size is approximately 66 centimeters high by 63 centimeters wide. The *nijiriguchi* said to have been built into the Taian tea room by Rikyû is comparatively large: 78 centimeters high by seventy-two centimeters wide. A rare few of the doors of *nijiriguchi* are hinged; the great majority of *nijiriguchi* have sliding doors. There are various theories about the origins of the nijiriguchi, but none has been accepted as definitive. While continuing our inquiries into the history of the *nijiriguchi*, we must also reflect upon the spiritual and conceptual purpose of having people crouch down in order to enter and leave the tea room.

Looking through the skylight window of the Yuin tea house,

we admire the greenery of the gingko tree planted by Sen Sôtan.

The radiant sun of early summer shines artfully through the window, and striking the leaves,

it flows through the spaces between them.

Its refracted glow diffuses through the *shôji*, providing a goodly amount of illumination.

Could Sôtan, who built Yuin and planted the gingko tree himself,

have imagined how his descendants hundreds of years later would employ this wordless art

constructed from nature and human artifice?

I am constantly impressed how all the configurations of the garden

and tea house at the Urasenke homestead assume uncontrived forms

that are respectful of nature and gently receptive of it.

And as I think about myself day and night within this bewildering modern-day life,

I am ever more determined to appreciate these uncontrived forms.

Uncontrived Forms

A Mountain Dwelling Within the City

The missionary João Rodrigues, in his *History of the Church in Japan*, wrote about a tea room and garden on a bustling city street that sought to recreate the separate world of a mountain hut. And in the text called *Nisuiki* there appears a description of the person living in such a hut as a "recluse (*inja*) within the city."

The *roji*, which plays an important role as the path leading to the tea house,

is also the source for the style of the Japanese garden as a "tea garden."

The *roji* with its hut is not only valuable as a place that accommodates pure self-training.

Its use of steppingstones and plantings that are not found in other gardens teaches us

the limitlessness of a space occupied by trees and rocks.

It evokes an atmosphere that combines philosophy, religion, and art,

an atmosphere in which you can immerse yourself in contemplative quietude.

An allegory from the *Lotus Sutra* speaks of

"Leaving this burning house of a world and living in a white garden (*byakuroji*)."

The *roji* is where your fundamental qualities are revealed in a state of complete nothingness.

The Garden *Roji*

The Garden

Among *roji*, there is the single-section garden with just the inner *roji*; the double-section garden with outer and inner *roji*; and the triple-section garden that has a middle *roji* constructed between the outer and inner *roji*. The basic features of the *roji* include shrubbery and steppingstones, middle gate and privy, and sword rack and water basin. There are two types of *roji*, the hut and *shoin* types. Because all *roji* are spaces that lead the guests to the tea room, they are designed to appear like mountain dwellings within the city, and it is prescribed that for the most part trees that blossom and trees that bear fruit should not be included among their plantings.

In general, the typical tea room is said to be four and a half mats in size. Originally, the tea room was called an "enclosure." At the time of the Buddha, Shákyamuni, there lived in India a devoted Buddhist layman, adept in religious practices, named Vimalakírti. We are told that his dwelling was exceedingly small—about ten-foot square, or roughly the size of a four-and-a-half-mat tea room.

The name *hôjô*, ten-foot square hut, for buildings at Buddhist temples came from this old story about Vimalakírti. At Zen temples in particular, it became the practice to refer to living quarters as hôjô. During the Muromachi period, *chanoyu* in a *shoin*-style room became fashionable. People divided eighteen-mat halls into four sections, each patterned after the hôjô-style dwelling of Vimalakírti. Enclosing the sections with folding screens, people were able freely to enjoy tea in them. These enclosures were the forerunners of the tea room. In Rikyû's time, the spirit of these enclosures was expressed in the designation of the four mats as spring, summer, autumn, and winter, and the half-mat as "the dog days of summer." There arose the idea, in accordance with *yin-yang* theory, of *taiza*, or opposite positions relating to the northern, southern, eastern, and western sides of the tea room. Four and a half mats is considered the standard measure of a drawing room.

The Hall (*Hiroma*) and Small Room (*Koma*)

Among tea rooms, those larger than four and a half mats are called *hiroma*, and those smaller are called *koma*. The four-and-a-half-mat room combines the functions of both the larger and smaller rooms. It is thought that the *hiroma* and *koma* derived from the *ôzashiki* (large drawing room) and *kozashiki* (small drawing room) of ancient times. It is possible, however, that at one time a six-mat drawing room was called *kozashiki*. But we cannot judge by just the size of a room. We must consider the thinking that lay behind tea rooms within the larger context of the way of tea as it has evolved until today, which is closely related to changes in tea practice and to a deepening of *wabi* tea.

Four and a Half Mats

The *Kaiseki* Meal and Sweets

The word *kaiseki* derives from the "Great Meditation in December": the strict exercises held

by the Zen sect of Buddhism from the first to the eighth of December each year.

These exercises are unusually strict even for a sect known for its strictness.

They are conducted in the quest of enlightenment (*satori*) on the very day—December 8—

when the Buddha became enlightened. The participants do not sleep, eat little food,

and, in the midst of the winter cold, engage in seated meditation.

They are sleepy, hungry, and cold beyond description.

In order to ease their coldness and hunger a little, the monks in training,

before commencing meditation, select appropriate stones, warm them,

and insert them into the folds of their *kimono* as substitute body-warmers.

The word *kaiseki* for the meal in *chanoyu* comes from this practice.

Its meaning is that the meal should not be extravagant:

it should consist, essentially, of one soup and three side dishes.

The *Kaiseki* Meal

The Formal *chanoyu* affair and the *Kaiseki* Meal

There are seven kinds of formal chanoyu affair: the morning gathering; the noontime gathering; the wintertime, after sundown gathering; the special, unscheduled gathering; the dawn gathering; the after-mealtime gathering; and the gathering for those unable to attend the morning or noontime gatherings. The meal that accompanies these gatherings is called the *kaiseki* meal. The principal purpose of the *kaiseki* meal is, above all, hospitality. Prescribed as consisting of one soup and three side dishes, it stresses quality rather than quantity. The host decides upon the menu not to satisfy his own tastes but with prime consideration for the likings of his guests. It is important that the food be seasonal. The host will go to great lengths to please his guests of that day as much as he can, taking into consideration their tastes and cultural backgrounds, their preferences in tea, their ages, where they are from, and so forth.

These days there are caterers that specialize in *kaiseki* cuisine.

But in earlier times the host planned the menu, selected the ingredients,

and did the cooking himself.

Planning the menu is itself one of the pleasures of holding a tea gathering.

The composition of the meal is determined by the guests invited,

the time of their arrival, and the season.

The meal was never extravagant; rather, the critical thing is for it to be as beautiful

and delicious as possible.

Such modest hospitality constitutes the spirit of the *kaiseki* meal.

The Spirit of
the *Kaiseki* Meal

Variety in the *Kaiseki* Meal

In general today, the following variety of things are served in the *kaiseki* meal: the *mukôzuke* appetizer; rice; soup; *wanmori* or cooked food in lacquered bowls; broiled food; light broth (*hashiarai*); dishes from the mountains and ocean on a square tray called *hassun*; hot water; and pickles. At times, *azukebachi* and *shiizakana*, or tidbits eaten with *sake*, are also served. While staying within this basic variety of things, the host, in accordance with the kind of gathering, gives careful attention to harmonizing the food and utensils with the season. He prepares his menu by giving primacy to what is tasty and easy to eat and by keeping in mind the order of things from the mountains and from the ocean.

Thick tea is the main point of a formal *chanoyu* affair;

hence both host and guests must maintain seriousness when engaged in this part of the affair.

Such an atmosphere draws together everything in the gathering and in the tea itself.

Accordingly, there is none of the freedom found in the serving of thin tea.

No cushions or smoking equipment are put out.

The guests do not engage in idle chatter among themselves,

and even the conversation between host and guests is minimal.

If those who become guests for thick tea are not versed in the conditions of *chanoyu*,

they will not understand the meaning of the activities

leading up to and following thick tea or the host's intentions.

Thick Tea *Koicha*

It is rare to find things that have such beautiful names as each and every item of Japanese confectionary. It is said that Japanese sweets are savored by the eyes, mouth, and ears. The ears are pleased by the names.

Of *wagashi* names, which are selected after very careful consideration, some are difficult to understand and some are easy.

The profound meanings attached to these sweets in the naming of them excellently match their colors, shapes, and tastes.

No doubt many of you had the experience as children of suffering aching legs in order to remain in formal seated position (*seiza*) and get sweets.

The slight, gentle flavor of *wagashi* is the ultimate in sweet taste, isn't it?

Some sweets last for days, but others soon lose their shapes.

Nothing matches *wagashi* as the embodiment of the "spirit of this very moment."

That is why I love these tender and charming sweets.

The Role of Japanese Sweets
Wagashi

Omogashi and *Higashi*

There are two types of sweets for tea gatherings: *omogashi* (prime sweets) and *higashi* (dried sweets). *Omogashi* include steamed sweets (*mushigashi*) and fresh sweets (*namagashi*), which are served with thick tea. They are rather soft. *Higashi* are served with thin tea, and include pressed and molded confections made from a type of sugar called *wasanbon* and rice powder, *arihei* candy, and *senbei*, crackers. There are times, during shortened gatherings when only thin tea is served, that both *omogashi* and *higashi* are served at the same time.

Concerning *Wabi*

"For those who await only the flowers,

show them the spring grasses emerging from the snow in a mountain village."

This is a poem by Fujiwara no Ietaka from the *Shin Kokin Waka Shû* anthology.

To people of the past, the poem expressed the spirit of the *wabi* aesthetic.

There are no flowers or crimson leaves, only a range of mountains covered white with snow.

Although spring will soon arrive, there is no sign of it.

Yet already nature in its vastness has begun to quicken its pace toward spring.

On the surface snow remains, but, within, the earth is about to bring forth new life.

I understand the feeling of discovering the world of *wabi* in such a setting.

One often finds the *wabi* spirit in tranquil society or in a lonely state of mind.

But people of old saw *wabi* in what they discerned to be movement beneath the snow,

and that makes me incomparably happy. I like it.

Wabi as a sign of movement directly expresses a characteristic of the Japanese people;

and I believe that foreigners also understand. If *wabi* were only loneliness, emptiness, and *yin*,

the most important essence of the way of tea would surely not have attained

its present level of perfection. Only when *wabi* becomes color and shines,

becomes wise and functions is there life in the way of tea.

Wabi Emerging

Afterword

Naya Sôtan

In 1954 I had the opportunity to travel with Hôunsai, then the heir apparent (*waka-sôshô*) of Urasenke. With the United States as our base, we visited Brazil, Peru, and other countries in Central and South America to spread the way of tea. That was my first trip abroad. For me, as one who was reserved and reluctant to travel, the decision to make the trip required, without exaggeration, a readiness to "jump off the verandah of Kiyomizu-dera Temple."

People are perverse by nature. When urged to go, they are uncertain whether or not they should; when held back and urged not to go, they unexpectedly wish to go. This was almost exactly how it was with me at that time.

I worried about Tankôsha, which was finally getting on track. But the desire to see foreign lands with my own eyes was strong. Although this was my first visit abroad, it wasn't a very elegant trip at all. We were literally overwhelmed with work every day.
Yet during this time, we were surrounded by *nisei*, filled with nostalgia and driven to tears just by hearing talk about Japan, who received with their hands together the tea that we prepared for them, and by other people of the countries we visited who relished powdered tea upon tasting it for the first time. Forgetting my fatigue, I felt all the more keenly the strength of tea.

Thereafter, as an aide to my older brother, the Grand Master Hôunsai, I have continued, through publishing, to spread the culture of the way of tea to a great many people. As a composite culture and composite art, the way of tea has brought together a variety of elements from the fine arts, architecture, and so on. And there are a great many books for the study and learning of each of these elements. However, at that time what we wished to convey in those lands that knew nothing of the way of tea was not how to prepare tea and handle its utensils, but the pure "the spirit of tea": that is, without dramatization or ornamentation, the honest "goodness of tea." I believe that, by means of our clumsy use of foreign languages and by body movements and hand gestures, we truly conveyed to people that spirit.

Even though we use the expression "the spirit of tea," it remains quite vague; and a sense of the "goodness of tea" is very difficult to convey. But by preparing a bowl of tea while looking into the eyes of the person for whom you are preparing it, you will communicate the tea spirit without words. I was able to attain the same noble experience as expressed by Sôtan in the old poem: "*Chanoyu* is conveyed to the heart, to the eyes, to the ears—with no need for written words."

I wish to transmit the "the spirit of tea" and the "goodness of tea" directly to people throughout the world. Through the medium of publication, I undertake to transmit these things to as many people as I can. I do this as a memorial service to the many who have gone before me, including my father Tantansai, my mother Seikôin, and my sister-in-law Jôkôin. Above all, I wish to repay my indebtedness to my older brother, Grand Master Hôunsai.

Grand Master Hôunsai has been spreading the way of tea abroad for fifty years, and has been Grand Master of Urasenke for forty years. The prose that he has cultivated for the purpose of spreading the way beautifully penetrates, without ornamentation or exaggeration, to the core of the tea spirit. Through this book, all readers will surely perceive that this spirit is not in some other place, but in the hearts and lives of each of them. Thus, the spirit of tea transcends differences of race and thought and climate to be shared by all the world—and continue to have universality.

I dream that people throughout the world who acquire this book will visit Japan and knock on the gate of the Grand Master.

Descriptions of the Photographs

The articles given in parentheses are from the Hosomi Museum.
The dry sweets shown in the photograph "Placing dry sweets on a folded paper" are named Aokaede, Taki, by Kameya Iori.

The Generations of Urasenke Grand Masters

The Founder, Sen no Sôeki

Called Rikyû. Born in Sakai 1522. Also called Hôsensai. Served Oda Nobunaga and given the surname Sen. Later served Toyotomi Hideyoshi. Studied Zen with Kokei Sôchin at Daitokuji Temple. Received the principles of tea from Takeno Jôô, and ultimately perfected the way of tea. Died on the twenty-eighth day of the second month of 1591 at age sixty-nine. At Urasenke, the memory of Rikyû is honored every year with a memorial service.

Second Generation, Shôan Sôjun

Heir to Rikyû. Mother, Sôon. Revived the Sen house, which had been discontinued following the death of Rikyû. Soon transferred the family headship to Sôtan. Retired to Saihôji Temple in the Nishiyama section of Kyoto. Died 1614 at age sixty-eight.

Third Generation, Genpaku Sôtan

Studied Zen with Shun'oku Sôen at Daitokuji Temple. Proclaimed that "Tea and Zen have the same flavor" (*chazen ichimi*). 1648 divided the Sen house into Urasenke and Omotesenke. As a leading person of culture of his day, he associated with many notable people. Died 1658 at age eighty. At Urasenke, a memorial service is held for Sôtan every year on November 19.

Fourth Generation, Sensô Sôshitsu

Called Rôgetsuan. Fourth son of Sôtan. Served Maeda Toshitsune of Kaga province, and spread the way of tea in the Hokuriku region. Made many contributions to the crafts: took Chôzaemon of Kyoto, a disciple of Raku Ichinyû, to Kaga and had him establish the Ôhi kiln; and he had Miyazaki Kanchi produce kettles. Died 1697 at age seventy-five.

Fifth Generation, Jôsô Sôshitsu

Called Fukyûsai. Son of Sensô. Served the Maeda of Kaga province and the Hisamatsu of Iyo province. Died 1704 at age thirty-one.

Sixth Generation, Taisô Sôan Sôshitsu

Because of the early death of Fukyûsai, he became family head at age ten. Called Rikkansai. Died 1726 at age thirty-two.

Seventh Generation, Chikusô Sôken Sôshitsu

Second son of Kakukakusai Gensô Sôsa of Omotesenke. Succeeded to the Urasenke headship, but died 1733 at age 24.

Eighth Generation, Ittô Sôshitsu

Younger brother of the seventh generation Grand Master, Chikusô, he succeeded as the eighth Grand Master of Urasenke. Called the restorer of the Sen house. Established the Seven Special Tea Exercises and left many favored tea articles. Also devoted much effort to the training of disciples, including Kanô Sôboku and Hayami Sôtatsu, founder of the Hayami School. Died 1771 at age fifty-two.

Ninth Generation, Sekiô Genshitsu Sôshitsu

Called Fukensai. His second son, Sekigyûsai (Daiô Sôgen), established a branch family, but died young. His third son, Sôjû, succeeded to the headship of Mushanokôjisenke as Kôkôsai Sôshu. Died 1801 at age fifty-five.

Tenth Generation, Nintokusai Sôshitsu

Oldest son of Fukensai. His wife, Sôkô, performed much meritorious work in the training of Gengensai in the way of tea. She performed many other important services as well. Nintokusai had no sons. His oldest daughter, Teruko, was a tea person called Genkasai or Kazan Sôhaku. Nintokusai died 1826 at age fifty-six.

Eleventh Generation, Gengensai Sôshitsu

The son of Matsudaira Noritomo of Mikawa province, he became Nintokusai's son-in-law. On the occasion of the two hundred and fiftieth memorial service for Rikyû, he renovated the tea rooms in his residence and added such tea rooms as Totsutotsusai, Dairo no Ma, Hôsensai, and Ryûseiken, giving shape to the present Urasenke. In addition, he wrote *Hogobusuma*, presenting to the public a guide for *temae*. He originated the style of tea employing seating furniture, and established the foundation for the modern way of tea. Moreover, as representative of the various schools of tea at the time, he petitioned the government to promote tea, claiming that it was not simply an elegant pastime (*yûgei*). Considered the restorer of the world of the way of tea. Called Seichû. Died 1877 at age sixty-seven.

Twelfth Generation, Yûmyôsai Genshitsu Sôshitsu

Second son of the Suminokura, a prominent Kyoto family. Married Gengensai's daughter, Yukako, and succeeded to the Urasenke family. His wife Yukako was called Shinseiin, and is well remembered for having spread the way of tea among women. Yûmyôsai died 1917 at age sixty-five.

Thirteenth Generation, Ennôsai Sôshitsu

Son of Yûmyôsai. Called Tetchû and Tairyû. Succeeded to the family headship at age eighteen. Faced with the crisis of the decline of traditional Japanese culture following the Meiji Restoration, he dedicated his life to its preservation and revival. Contributed to the modernization of the way of tea by establishing the summer seminar and by introducing the way to school curricula. Died 1924 at age fifty-two. His wife Tsunako devoted herself wholeheartedly to assisting Ennôsai. She died a year later, 1925.

Fourteenth Generation, Tantansai Sôshitsu

Son of Ennôsai. Mugensai. Succeeded to the family headship 1923. Beginning with the formal presentation of tea to Empress Teimei, he was active in such presentations to other members of the imperial family and to prominent foreign visitors. Was also active in the formal presentation of tea at Shinto shrines and Buddhist temples, thus opening a new avenue to the world of tea. Became doyen of the entire world of tea, exerting his leadership therein. Dispatched Hôunsai, the present Grand Master, to propagate the way of tea abroad, thus establishing the basis for its current flourishing there. Also demonstrated his foresight institutionally. Seeking the consolidation of Urasenke's way of tea, he formed Tankôkai. Among his many contributions to tea, he devoted himself to spreading the way through numerous publications. He was the first person of tea to receive the Medal of Honor With Purple Ribbon from the Emperor. Died suddenly in 1964 at age seventy.

His wife Kayako was a great help to Tantansai behind the scenes. As an active member of the Soroptimists, she contributed to the spread of the way of tea internationally. Died 1980 at age eighty-one.

Fifteenth Generation, Grand Master Hôunsai Sôshitsu

Present Grand Master of Urasenke. Oldest son of Tantansai. Made first trip to the United States to introduce the way of tea in 1951. Subsequently has made more than 250 trips to more than fifty countries throughout the world. In addition to spreading the way of tea as a form of traditional Japanese culture throughout the world, he founded the Urasenke Professional College of the Way of Tea (Urasenke Gakuen Chadô Senmon Gakkô) with the aim of training successors to the tea world; and in 1994 he opened the Urasenke Junior College for the Way of Tea (Urasenke Chadô Tanki Daigaku) at the University of Commerce in Tianjin, China. Moreover, to advance the way of tea academically, he has worked to establish *chadô* as a discipline by teaching at many universities in Japan and abroad. Has also participated actively in Rotary International, the international service organization. Has literally served as the "face of Japan." In 1997 he became the first person of the world of tea to receive the Order of Culture from the Emperor. Thus has he been active as a representative of Japanese culture.

His wife Tomiko supported his activities behind the scenes. She also served in many public positions as the Japanese representative of the Soroptimists International. Her contributions to the world of education were particularly great. As mother of the Urasenke clan, she became a pillar of the spirit of the world of *chadô*. Died suddenly in 1999 at age sixty-seven, widely lamented.

Urasenke Branch Offices and Liaison Offices Abroad

Australia
Urasenke Brisbane Liaison Office
23 Ruskin Street,Taringa
Brisbane, Queensland
AUSTRALIA 4068

Urasenke Sydney Branch
130/19-23 Herbert Street
St. Leonards. N. S. W.
AUSTRALIA 2065

Brazil
Uraenke Brazil Branch
Rua Tamandare 272, Apt. 51-B
Liberdade, Sao Paulo
BRAZIL CEP 01525-000

Canada
Urasenke Vancouver Branch
3953 W. 13th Ave.
Vancouver, B. C.
CANADA V6R 2T1

China
Urasenke Beijing Branch
P. O. Box 70 No.111
Beijing Foreign Studices University
2 North Xisanhuan Avenue
Beijing
CHINA 100081

Urasenke Tianjin
Junior College of Urasenke Way of Tea
Tianjin University of Commerce
East Entrance of Jimba Road
Northern Suburbs of Tianjin
CHINA 300400

England
Urasenke London Branch
4 Langton Way
Blackheath, London SE3 7TL
ENGLAND

France
Urasenke Paris Branch
Fondation Urasenke
Tour Palerme, App. 12-11
142 Bd. Massena
Paris 75013
FRANCE

Germany
Urasenke Dusseldorf Branch
Niederkasseler Kirchweg 150
40547 Dusseldorf
GERMANY

Urasenke Freiburg Liaison Office
Hans-Jakobstr. 26A
79194 Gundelfingen
GERMANY

Italy
Urasenke Rome Branch
Centro Urasenke
Via Giovanni Nicotera 29
Rome
ITALY

Korea
Urasenke Chado Cultural Exchange Society
Hae-Young Building. 7th Floor, Room 710
148 Ankuk-Dong, Jungro-Gu
Seoul
KOREA

Mexico
Uraesnke Mexico Branch
Fuego 691
Col. Jardines del Pedregal
01900 Mexico D. F.
MEXICO

The Netherlands
Urasenke Netherlands Liaison Office
Gijsbrecht van Amstellaan 5
1181 EJ Amstelveen
THE NETHERLANDS

Russia
Urasenke Moscow Liaison Office
Naberijunaya
Shufechenko Street
D. 3. Room No.31
Moscow
RUSSIA

United States of America
Urasenke Hawaii Branch
245 Saratoga Road
Honolulu, HI 96815
U. S. A.

Urasenke New York Branch
Urasenke Chanoyu Center
153 East 69th Street
New York, NY 10021
U. S. A.

Urasenke San Francisco Branch
2143 Powell Street
San Francisco, CA 94133
U. S. A.

Urasenke Seattle Branch
1910 37th Place East
Seattle, WA 98112
U. S. A.

Urasenke Washington D. C. Branch
6930 Hector Road
McLean, VA 22101
U. S. A.

As of June 2002